MI FAMILIA CALACA

MY SKELETON FAMILY

CYNTHIA WEILL

PAPER MACHE BY
JESÚS CANSECO ZÁRATE

Hi, I'm Anita.
Let me introduce my family.
I'm the big sister.

....

Hola, soy Anita.
Les presento a mi familia.
Yo soy la hermana mayor.

My brother Miguel.
He's a brat.

....

Mi hermano Miguel.
Él es muy travieso.

Juanito is the baby.
He's so cute!

....

Juanito es el bebé.
¡Él es tan lindo!

Us kids.

....

Nosotros los niños.

My beautiful mother.

....

Mi hermosa mamá.

My handsome father.

....

Mi guapo papá.

My parents.
They are the greatest!

....

Mis papás.
¡Son fantásticos!

My grandmother.
She gives me good advice.

....

Mi abuelita.
Me da muy buenos consejos.

My grandfather.
He's so sweet.

....

Mi abuelito.
Él es tan tierno.

My grandparents.
They are the best.

....

Mis abuelitos.
Mis abuelos son los mejores.

My great-grandmother.
She tells wonderful stories.

. . . .

Mi bisabuela.
Ella cuenta cuentos
maravillosos.

The pets.
My best friends!

....

Las mascotas.
¡Son mis mejores amigos!

The men of my family.

....

Los hombres de mi familia.

The women of my family.

....

Las mujeres de mi familia.

My wonderful family.
I love them a lot!

....

Mi maravillosa familia.
¡Quiero mucho a mi familia!

In Mexico the skeleton is a beloved and humorous figure.
Its origins go back to pre-Columbian times.

To my dear friend Joyce Grossbard. This book would never have been made without
your nurturing spirit and generosity. —Cindy

A mi madre Ana María Canseco que me ha apoyado y ha creído en mí y mis locuras. —Jesús

Photographer: David Hilbert

Thanks to: Stephanie Villarreal, Michael Donnelly, Jan Asikainen, Chloe Sayer, Olga
Hubard, Christine Brown, Sarah Thompson, Emanuelle Guyon, Harry Baudouin,
Ophelia and May Chapman, Nancy Mygatt, Ruth Borgman, Janet Glass, Anne
Mayagoitia, Ruth Meyers, Vicky Weill, José Miguel Moracho, Bessy Reyna, Myriam
Chapman, Museo Estatal de Arte Popular de Oaxaca, Bank Street Writers Lab, and
Friends of Oaxacan Folk Art.

La Familia: A Mexican Folk Art Family in English and Spanish. Copyright © 2013 by Cynthia Weill.
All rights reserved. No part of this book may be used or reproduced in any manner whatsoever without
written consent from the publisher, except for brief quotations for reviews. For further information, write
Cinco Puntos Press, 701 Texas Avenue, El Paso, TX 79901; or call 1-915-838-1625.
FIRST EDITION 10 9 8 7 6 5 4 3 2 1
Library of Congress Cataloging-in-Publication Data
Weill, Cynthia. Mi familia calaca = My skeleton family / by Cynthia Weill ; figures by Jesus Canseco
Zarate. -- FIRST EDITION. pages cm
Summary: "Welcome to the Family! It's just like yours: father, mother, sister, brother, abuelita, gato. Well,
but, there's something just a little bit different about this family. Maybe it's those clothes they wear…just a
little bit fashion backward. And the colors! So vibrant and… lively. Maybe that's what it is. They are just so
full of life. Familia-life from a Day of the Dead perspective!"—Provided by publisher.
English and Spanish. ISBN 978-1-935955-50-4 (hardback)
1. Paper-mache sculpture—Mexico—Juvenile literature. 2. All Soul's Day in art—Juvenile literature. 3.
Families in art—Juvenile literature. I. Zárate, Jesús Canseco, illustrator. Sculpture. Selections. II. Title.
III. Title: My skeleton family. NK8555.5.M64Z372 2013, 745.54'2—dc23
2013012342